STEP-BY-STEP

MAKING CARDS

CHARLOTTE STOWELL

ILLUSTRATED BY JIM ROBINS

Kingfisher

NEW YORK

KINGFISHER
Larousse Kingfisher Chambers Inc.
95 Madison Avenue
New York, New York 10016

First American edition, 1995

10 9 8 7 6 5 4 3 2 1 (RLB)
10 9 8 7 6 5 4 3 2 1 (PB)

LIBRARY OF CONGRESS
CATALOGING-IN-PUBLICATION DATA
Stowell, Charlotte.
    Making cards/Charlotte Stowell.
    —1st American ed.
       p.   cm. — (Step by step)
    1. Greeting cards. Juvenile literature.
    I. Title. II. Series:
Step-by-step (Kingfisher Books)
TT872.S85 1992
745.594 1—dc20   94-47818 CIP AC

ISBN 1-85697-591-6 (RLB)
ISBN 1-85697-590-8 (PB)

Series editor: Deri Robins
Series designer: Ben White
Illustrator: Jim Robins
Photographer: Steve Shott
Cover designer: Terry Woodley

Printed in Hong Kong

CONTENTS

WHAT YOU NEED

To make the cards in this book, collect together a basic kit like the one shown here. Some of the projects require a few extra bits and pieces—check by reading through the step-by-step instructions before you begin.

Glue

Scissors

The Basics

The main thing you'll need is a supply of thin cardboard. Heavy paper can also work well. If you use thin paper, fold each sheet in half to double the thickness—otherwise they'll be too floppy to stand up!

Colored tissue, crepe, wrapping paper, old magazines, and wallpaper can all be used to decorate your cards.

Felt-tip pens

Dried beans and lentils

Foam block

Square

Tools of the Trade

You'll need a pair of scissors, a square, a craft knife, a metal ruler, paintbrushes, pencils, and a cutting board to protect your table—a big piece of cardboard, wood, or Formica is ideal.

Always handle craft knives very carefully, and only use them when an adult is around to help.

Paints and Glue

For sticking paper and cardboard together, use ordinary white glue or paper paste.

Most of the cards in this book were decorated by cutting shapes out of paper and gluing them to the design. You could also color your cards with paints or felt-tip pens.

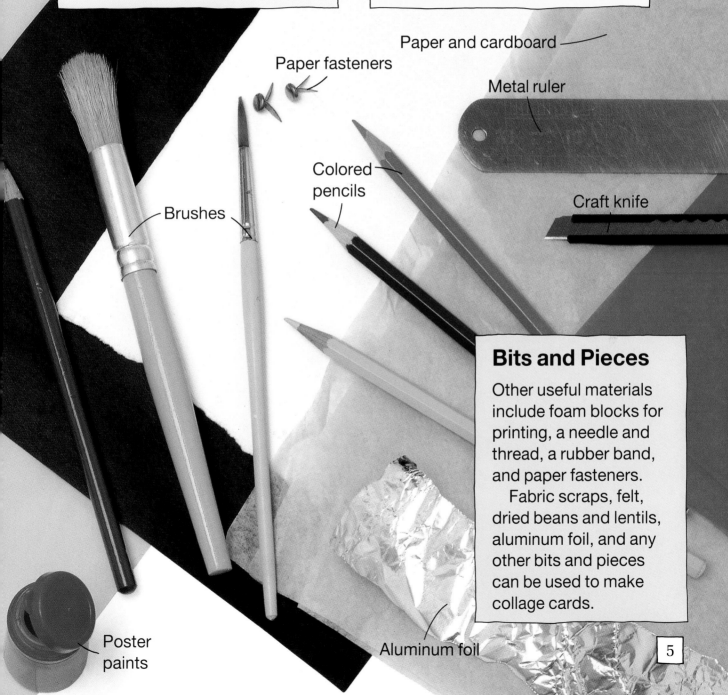

Paper fasteners

Paper and cardboard

Metal ruler

Colored pencils

Craft knife

Brushes

Bits and Pieces

Other useful materials include foam blocks for printing, a needle and thread, a rubber band, and paper fasteners.

Fabric scraps, felt, dried beans and lentils, aluminum foil, and any other bits and pieces can be used to make collage cards.

Poster paints

Aluminum foil

HINTS AND TIPS

The cards in this book are all easy to make—
they're also a lot more fun to send than ones
you've bought from a store! Just take your time,
and follow all the instructions carefully. Before
you start, read the tips below.

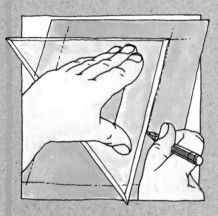

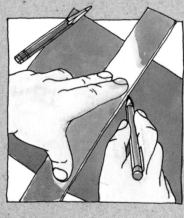

Measuring

It's best to use a square
rather than a ruler when
you're measuring your
cards. If you use the
right-angled edges to
help you draw the
corners, your cards
will look very
professional.

Folding

Folding cardboard is
easier if you *score* it
first. Measure and draw
the fold line using a
ruler and a pencil. Then
press the nib of an
empty ballpoint pen
along the line, using a
metal ruler as a guide.

Illustrating

To illustrate your cards,
you could simply paint
a design on the front.
Or, cut shapes from
colored paper and
glue them down. You
can even make collage
cards, using all kinds of
bits and pieces.

*The pictures on the right show three different
ways of illustrating the same design. Each
illustration was done on a separate piece of
cardboard, then cut and glued onto a piece of
folded cardboard. This is called "mounting."*

Painted card

Collage card,
made with felt,
beans, and seeds

Card decorated
with paper
shapes

PRINTING CARDS

Use small shapes to print borders. They are also a good way to build up pictures—for example, a simple oval shape was repeated to make the petals of the sunflower opposite.

1

Draw a simple shape onto a piece of thick Styrofoam using a felt-tip pen. Cut the shape out carefully with a craft knife.

2

Cut several squares from thin cardboard or construction paper, each a little smaller than the folded cards you have already prepared.

Printing is a quick way to make a big batch of cards—at Christmas, for example, or when you want to invite a lot of friends to a party. Before you start printing, cut out all the cards you need. Fold them in half and put them to one side.

Pour some poster paint into a saucer. Dip the printing shape into the paint and press it firmly onto one of the squares.

Keep dipping and printing until you have enough pictures. When they're dry, mount them onto the front of the folded cards.

MAKING ENVELOPES

Your cards will look extra special if you send them in your own homemade envelopes! The instructions given here will work for any size. Try printing the backs and borders with brightly colored paints (see pages 8–9) and sealing the flaps with glue or stickers.

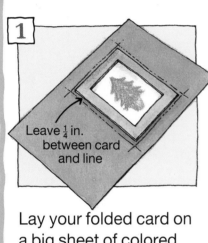

1

Leave ¼ in. between card and line

Lay your folded card on a big sheet of colored paper. Draw around it, making the line ¼ inch wider on all sides.

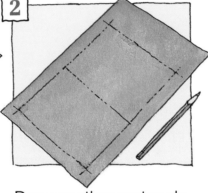

2

Draw another rectangle under the first one. It should be exactly the same width, but about ¼ inch shorter.

Why send plain envelopes when printed ones look so terrific?

3

¾ in.

Draw curves inside the bottom two corners. Add two ¾-inch flaps at each side of the top rectangle, as shown.

4

Draw a triangle at the top, making it at least 2 inches deep so that it overlaps the bottom rectangle when folded.

2 in.

5

Glue flaps

Cut out the shape with a craft knife. Fold all the lines inward, and glue the bottom rectangle over the side flaps.

BIRTHDAY SHAPES

Here are some very simple cards that just need a little folding and cutting. The colorful numbers would make great birthday cards for friends, brothers, or sisters—or how about making the leaping dolphin for an animal-loving mom or dad?

1

Folded edge

2

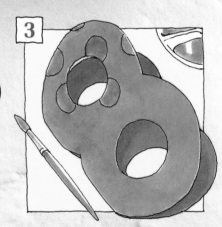

3

Number Cards

Draw a number onto a piece of folded cardboard. One side must touch the fold.

Cut out the number, making sure you don't cut through the folded part of the design.

Paint the card, or decorate it by gluing down shapes cut from colored paper.

Stand-ups

Cut out a rectangle from cardboard and lightly pencil a line across the middle.

Draw a design with the top part just above the middle line. Color with paints or paper collage.

Cut around the top part with a craft knife. Then score along the line and fold backward.

The train was made in the same way as the number cards, but the folded edge is at the top, not at the side.

The ark and dolphin both have a simple stand-up shape that can easily be cut out with a craft knife.

SURPRISE!

Always keep the main picture of a surprise card hidden—just hint at what's underneath, as we've done here with the tip of the tiger's ears!

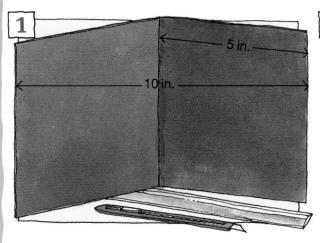

1

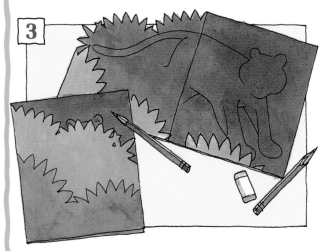

5 in.

10 in.

Measure a 10 x 5-inch rectangle onto a piece of green cardboard and cut it out. Score a line down the middle and fold the card in half.

2

Draw a simple bush shape on the front of the card, as shown in the picture. Cut along this line, using a craft knife or scissors.

3

Close the card and lightly sketch the tip of the tiger's ears on the inside, using a pencil. Open the card again, and draw the rest of the tiger's body.

4

Use paints or pieces of colored paper to decorate the inside and outside of the card. Write your message on the back.

Secret Message

Cut a dog's body out of colored paper and glue it to the front of a folded piece of cardboard. Draw and cut out the dog's head, and glue just the top part to the card.

Make a tiny envelope (pages 10–11), tuck in a secret message, and stick it under the dog's chin!

PUZZLE CARDS

The pictures on these cards are magically revealed when the pieces are put in the right order or when the dots are joined together!

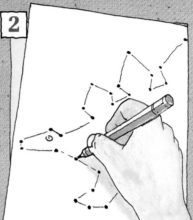

Dot-to-Dot

Lightly draw a simple design onto a piece of paper, using a pencil.

Use a felt-tip pen to mark clear dots along the pencil line.

Number the dots in the correct order. Erase the pencil marks and mount the picture onto a card.

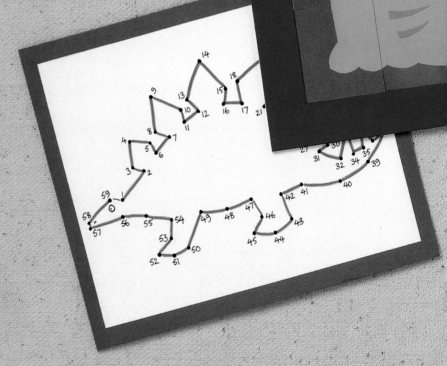

Jigsaw Card

1 Draw a rectangle measuring 7 x 6 inches onto a piece of cardboard. Cut it out.

2 Draw a border ¾ inch inside the edge of the cardboard. Cut along border to make a frame.

3 Place the frame on another piece of cardboard. Draw along the inside with a pencil, and cut this out.

4 Turn this piece of cardboard into a picture using paints or paper collage, then cut it into simple jigsaw pieces.

5 Fold a 12 x 7-inch piece of cardboard in half and glue the frame to the front. Send in an envelope, along with the jigsaw pieces.

POP-UP CARDS

These cards look terrific, and they're easy to make when you know how! You can change the picture to suit any kind of theme—just follow all the measurements given here.

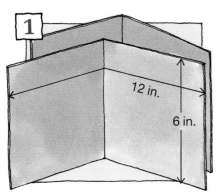

1 Take two pieces of thin cardboard, each 12 x 6 inches. Score and fold both pieces of cardboard down the middle.

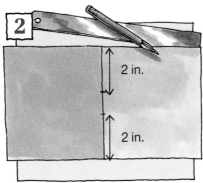

2 On one of the pieces, measure 2 inches along the fold from either edge, and mark the two points with a pencil.

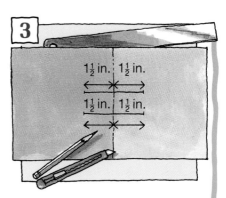

3 Draw a 3-inch line through each of these points ($1\frac{1}{2}$ inches on either side of the fold). Cut along both lines.

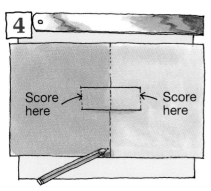

4 Now lightly score two lines between the cut lines, as shown.

5 Close and open the card, making the center strip fold inward.

6 Decorate the background with paints or paper collage.

7 On a new piece of cardboard, draw a pop-up shape that will fit inside the card.

8 Cut out and decorate the pop-up shape. Glue it to the lower half of the center strip, as shown.

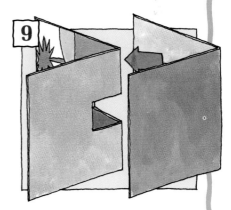

9 Glue the other piece of cardboard to the back —but don't put any glue on the center strip!

ZIGZAG CARDS

Fold, cut, and unfold—and a whole herd of elephants appears! Try cutting out a different design and you have a row of teddy bears, or a little train . . . .

The tomato card has a special surprise tucked into its front pocket—a pack of seeds that grow into beautiful plants!

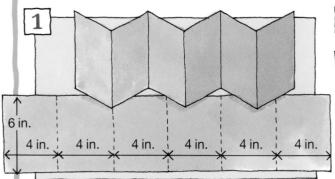

1

6 in.

4 in. | 4 in. | 4 in. | 4 in. | 4 in. | 4 in.

Take a strip of thin cardboard, measuring 24 by 6 inches. Divide it into six 4-inch sections with a ruler and pencil. Score along the lines, then fold the card into a zigzag.

2

At least ½ in.

Draw your design onto the front of the folded strip. Make sure the design touches both sides of the card for at least ½ inch at each point, or it will all fall apart when you cut it out!

3

Cut out the design, then carefully unfold it again. Paint one side of the card, or glue down shapes cut from colored paper. Write your message on the back of the card.

Say It With Seeds!

Buy a pack of seeds. Cut and fold a zigzag (make it a little bigger than the pack). Cut a cardboard pocket for the seeds and glue it to the front.

On the inside, show what happens when you plant the seeds!

TOMATO

TOMATO

MOBILES

Yet another brilliant idea that's a lot easier than it looks. This type of card is very eye-catching because the mobile shape keeps swinging around in even the gentlest breeze.

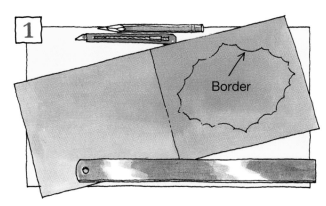

1 Cut out a rectangle of cardboard, and score a line down the middle. Draw a border on the front—the cards in the photo should give you some ideas.

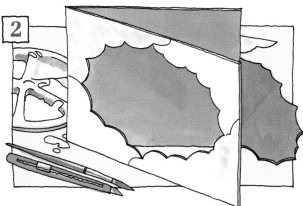

2 Cut out the part inside the border and fold the card in half. Paint the front and insides of the card, or decorate them with paper shapes.

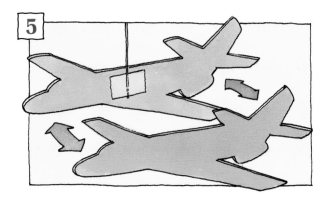

3 Cut out a shape from another piece of cardboard. Make sure that it fits within the border. Draw around it to make a second shape and cut this out, too.

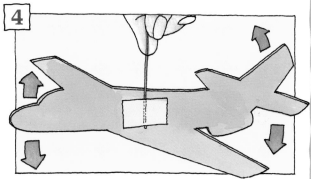

4 Cut a piece of thread about 3 inches long. Tape it lightly to one of the shapes—alter the position until the shape balances from the thread.

5 Glue the second shape over the first so that the thread is trapped between them. Decorate both sides of the shape with paints or paper collage.

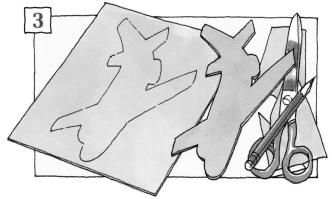

6 Tape the top of the thread inside the front of the card. Check that the shape can swing around without touching the border.

MOVING PICTURES

Pull the tab and watch the balloon glide across the sky! For this design, you'll need one piece of cardboard measuring 8 x 6 inches and another measuring $16\frac{1}{2}$ x $6\frac{1}{2}$ inches. You'll also need to cut out a narrow strip, 10 inches long and 1 inch wide.

1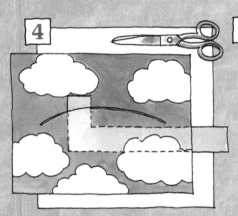

Cut a curved slot in the smaller piece of cardboard using a saucer as a guide. Leave 1 inch on both edges.

2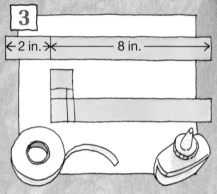

Decorate this piece, avoiding the curve. Draw and decorate the balloon on another piece, and cut it out.

3

Cut the narrow strip into two pieces. Glue the pieces into an "L" shape, and tape over the corner.

4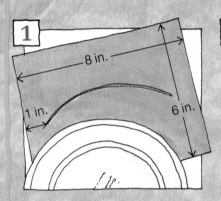

When the glue is dry, tuck the shorter length of the "L" through the slot from behind, as shown in the picture.

5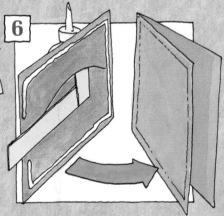

Glue the balloon to the top of the "L" shape. Check that it moves freely when you pull the other end of the strip.

6

Fold the larger piece of cardboard, and glue the decorated piece to the front. Don't put glue near the "L" strip.

The winged horse flies across the sky in
the same way as the balloon.
You could also try drawing a
bird, a plane . . . or even
your favorite
superhero!

CARDS WITH FEET!

These cute 3-D cards can be folded flat for sending. The methods shown here can be adapted to make animals of all shapes and sizes—how about a tall giraffe, a plump hippo, or even a whole team of reindeer for Christmas?

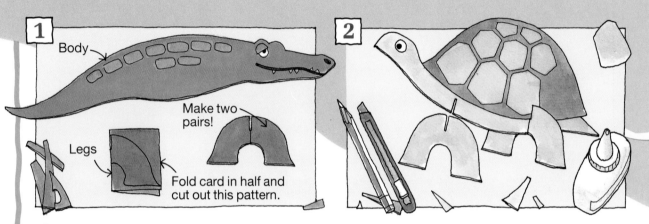

1

Body

Legs

Make two pairs!

Fold card in half and cut out this pattern.

2

Crocodile and Turtle

Draw the turtle or crocodile's body onto stiff cardboard, and cut it out. Make two pairs of legs as shown.

Cut two $\frac{1}{2}$-inch slots in the body, and one into the top of each pair of legs. Decorate, and slot in the legs.

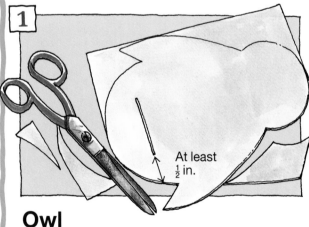

1

At least $\frac{1}{2}$ in.

2

Fold over to make tail

Owl

Draw the body onto cardboard and cut it out. Cut a slot across the bottom half, leaving at least $\frac{1}{2}$ inch between the slot and each edge.

Cut out and fold a shape like the one above for the feet and tail. Slot this through the body. Decorate the owl using paints or paper collage.

Decorate one side of your animal card using paints or paper shapes. Then write your message on the other side—use a fountain pen, a colored felt-tip, or, best of all, a gold or silver pen.

WINDOW CARDS

"Stained glass" cards look beautiful and mysterious—they're often made at Christmastime, but there's nothing to stop you from sending them in spring, summer, or fall!

1

Cut out a 6¾-inch square of cardboard. Draw a design onto the front, leaving at least ¾ inch between it and the edge. Leave "bridges" of at least ⅓ inch between the holes.

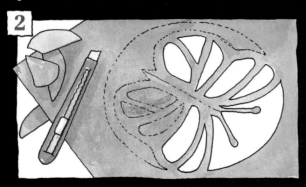

2

Cut out the holes for the "window-panes" with a craft knife. If you cut through a bridge by mistake, fix it with tape.

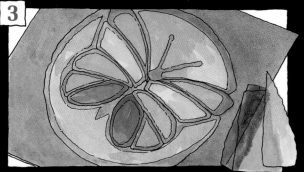

Cut the windowpanes from pieces of colored tissue paper or crepe paper. Put glue on one side of the cardboard and stick down the colored pieces—trim them so they don't overlap.

Fold a $15\frac{1}{3}$ x $7\frac{3}{4}$-inch piece of cardboard in half. Draw a $\frac{3}{4}$-inch border onto the front and cut out the middle. Glue your stained glass window to the back, as shown.

ZODIAC COLLAGE

Most of the cards in this book were decorated by gluing down pieces of colored paper. However, you could also use old magazines, newspapers, aluminum foil, postcards, stamps, scraps of fabric or wallpaper, dried beans or pasta, flowers or grasses, shells, nuts and bolts . . . the possibilities are endless!

Here's how to make a zodiac card from collage. There is a design for every star sign! Copy the shapes onto cardboard, or ask an adult to enlarge them on a photocopier.

1

Cut and fold a piece of cardboard—as big or as little as you like. Draw one of the zodiac signs onto the front. If you're using a photocopy, cut it out and glue it down.

2

Sort out the materials you're going to use. Put glue on the design, a little at a time, and gradually cover it with your materials. Leave it to dry before sending.

Capricorn

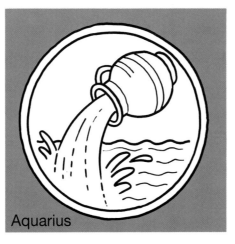

Aquarius

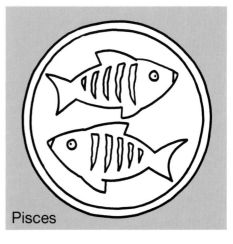

Pisces

Aries

Taurus

Gemini

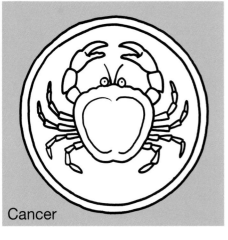

Cancer

Leo

Virgo

Libra

Scorpio

Sagittarius

CHRISTMAS CARDS

At Christmastime, when you need to make a big batch of cards, the best idea is to set up a printing press and go into mass-production!

For a few special people, try making the cat-in-a-stocking to hang on the tree—or turn the page to discover how to make a jolly Santa who jumps right out of the envelope!

Printed Cards

Follow the instructions for printing cards on pages 8–9. Print simple shapes such as a tree, a present, or a star.

While your printing press is up and running, why not make your own wrapping paper—use wallpaper or brown wrapping paper.

Use scraps of cardboard for gift tags. Make holes with a hole punch, and thread with ribbon.

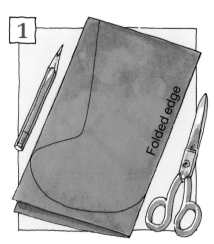

Christmas Cat

Fold a piece of thin, colored cardboard in half. Draw the stocking shape, with the folded edge as one side. Cut it out.

Glue the edges of the stocking together, but leave the top open. Draw and cut out a cat from black cardboard. Glue it in the stocking.

Decorate the card with bits of colored paper. Tape a loop of ribbon to the back, and write your Christmas greeting underneath.

All kinds of simple Christmas shapes can be used for your prints and tree decorations. How about stars, holly, snowpeople, or angels?

33

Pop-up Santa

Copy the diagram (shown right) onto a piece of red cardboard, using a pencil and ruler. Paint or decorate Santa's head and the chimney section.

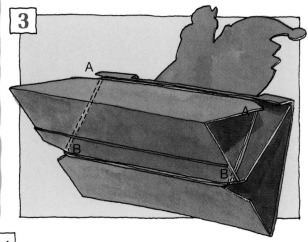

Score and fold the cardboard in along the dotted lines, and tuck the Santa through the middle slit. The folded card should form a shape like the one shown in step 3.

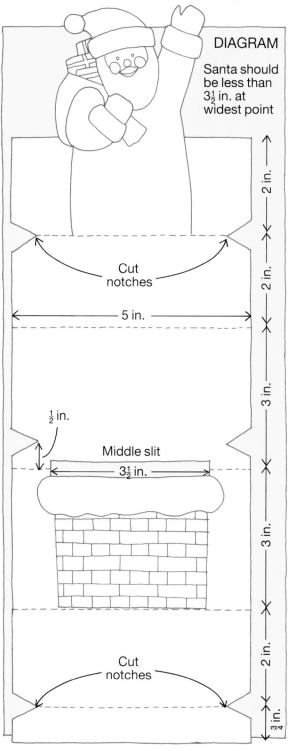

DIAGRAM

Santa should be less than 3½ in. at widest point

2 in.

Cut notches

2 in.

5 in.

3 in.

½ in.

Middle slit

3½ in.

3 in.

Cut notches

2 in.

¾ in.

Loop one end of a rubber band over the notches at the back (A), and loop the opposite end over the notches at the bottom (B). This may look tricky, but it's very simple once you get the hang of it!

4

To put the card into the envelope, gently squeeze the sides until it is flat.

When someone opens the envelope, the rubber band makes the Santa pop back up!

Here's a stylish valentine to make for the one you love (don't forget to add your secret message on the back)!

Start by cutting out a rectangle of colored cardboard measuring 7 x 4¾ inches. Then cut out a square of cardboard in another color measuring 4¾ x 4¾ inches.

Try dangling a tiny heart on a piece of thread inside the main shape.

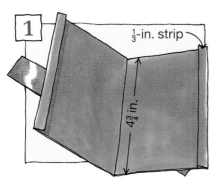

1

Score and fold the larger piece of cardboard down the middle. Then score a $\frac{1}{3}$-inch strip at each side and fold the strips toward you.

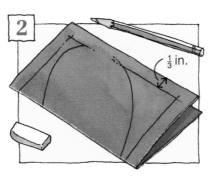

2

Fold the smaller piece in half. Draw a border $\frac{1}{3}$ inch from the edges. Draw half of a heart shape, making the sides touch the border.

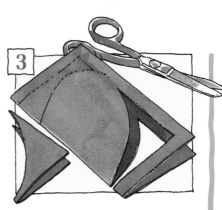

3

Cut out the area around the heart or, for a slightly different card, just cut out the heart. Both types are shown in the photo.

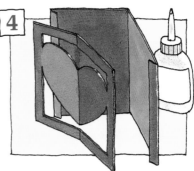

4

Glue the sides of the card to the folded strips on the larger card. Leave to dry before folding again.

To make a pair of tiny hearts, just cut out a single heart from the middle of the folded smaller card.

37

EASTER CHICKS

When you open the top half of this Easter egg, a bright yellow chick hatches out!

You'll need cardboard measuring $4\frac{1}{3}$ x 3 inches for each egg, and a 4-inch square of yellow cardboard for the chick. You'll also need a paper fastener to hold the egg together.

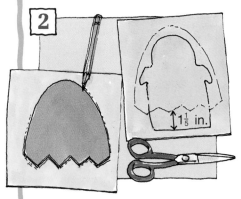

1

Cut out an egg shape from colored cardboard. Cut a zigzag across the middle.

If fluffy chicks don't appeal, how about a baby dinosaur?

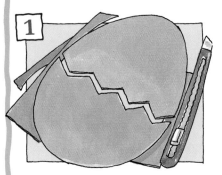

2

1⅕ in.

Place the top of the egg on the yellow square, and draw around it. Draw the chick inside the line, adding an extra $1\frac{1}{5}$ inch onto the bottom. Cut out the chick.

3

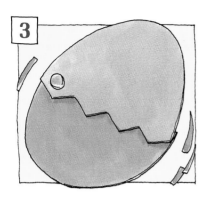

Overlap the two egg halves, and join them at one side with a paper fastener. Close the egg, and trim the edges to make a neat shape.

4

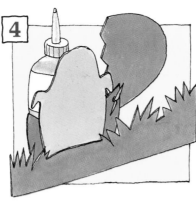

Glue the chick to the back of the bottom half of the egg. Cut out a strip of "grass," and glue this behind the bottom of the egg.

5

Cut and fold a 12½ x 5½-inch piece of cardboard. Glue the grass strip, the chick, and the bottom half of the egg to the front of the card.

Instead of step 5, you could make your egg stand up by itself—just glue a folded piece of cardboard to the back.

MORE IDEAS

You don't have to wait for a special occasion to send a card—it's a good way to keep in touch all year round!

Writing thank you letters doesn't have to be boring! Cut out a little card in the shape of the gift—then just scribble your note of thanks on the back.

Moving? Make some cards to let your friends know where your new home is!

Paper fastener

Pack some blank postcards and your paints or felt-tip pens next time you go on vacation— homemade postcards are a lot nicer than ones you can buy from souvenir shops!